Stories of Everyday Things

# The Story of TOILET PAPER

by Gloria Koster

PEBBLE
a capstone imprint

Published by Pebble, an imprint of Capstone
1710 Roe Crest Drive, North Mankato, Minnesota 56003
capstonepub.com

Copyright © 2025 by Capstone. All rights reserved. No part of this publication may be reproduced in whole or in part, or stored in a retrieval system, or transmitted in any form or by any means, electronic, mechanical, photocopying, recording, or otherwise, without written permission of the publisher.

Library of Congress Cataloging-in-Publication Data is available on the Library of Congress website.
ISBN: 9780756582036 (hardcover)
ISBN: 9780756582210 (paperback)
ISBN: 9780756582050 (ebook PDF)

Summary: Toilet paper often goes overlooked—until you need it! Who invented this household staple? How is it made? And how does it end up in homes and bathrooms around the world? Learn the answers and unravel the history of toilet paper in this informational book.

Editorial Credits
Editor: Alison Deering; Designer: Jaime Willems; Media Researcher: Jo Miller; Production Specialist: Whitney Schaefer

Image Credits
Alamy: Historic Collection, 12; Getty Images: Evgeny Kharitonov, 15, Grace Cary, 7, ImagineGolf, 14, industryview, 24, shaunl, 22; Shutterstock: Alzay, 21, DCStockPhotography, 13, DedMityay, 18, 23, ehrlif, 10, Fototocam, 6, goldenporshe, 25, grey_and, Cover (toilet paper bottom right), Johan Larson, 27, Marius GODOI, 29, Moreno Soppelsa, 16, Naparat, 5, Nataly Studio, Cover (toilet paper top), NavyBank, 26, Quang Ho, Cover (empty toilet roll), Russ Heinl, 17, seeshooteatrepeat, 19, slexp880, 20, Suprachai Akkho, Cover (crumpled tissue), Tony Moran, 9, Volodymyr_Shtun, 11, Yuliya D'yakova, 4; SuperStock: Artokoloro, 8

Design Elements: Shutterstock: Luria, Pooretat moonsana

Any additional websites and resources referenced in this book are not maintained, authorized, or sponsored by Capstone. All product and company names are trademarks™ or registered® trademarks of their respective holders.

# Table of Contents

What Is Toilet Paper?.................................4

Early Bathroom Behavior ......................... 8

From Forest to Factory...........................14

Earth-Friendly Toilet Paper.....................22

Make Your Own
Toilet Paper Planters ...........................28

Glossary.............................................30

Read More ..........................................31

Internet Sites ......................................31

About the Author ................................32

Index .................................................32

**Words in bold appear in the glossary.**

# What Is Toilet Paper?

Toilet paper keeps our bottoms clean. It is an important part of good **hygiene**. But what is toilet paper?

Toilet paper is a long strip of soft paper. Usually, the strip is wrapped around a cardboard tube. Rows of tiny holes separate the paper into sheets. These holes make the paper easy to tear.

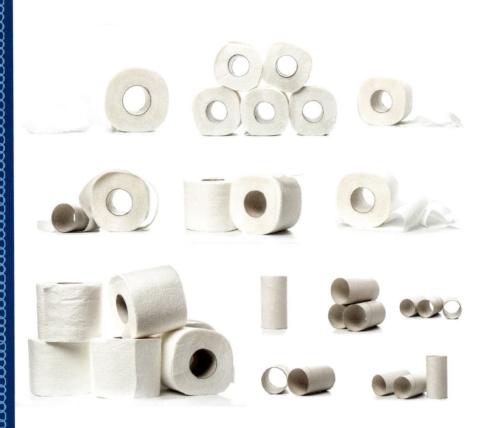

Toilet paper rolls can be big or small. The paper can also be different. One-**ply** toilet paper has a single layer of paper. Two-ply is thicker. It is stronger. It soaks up **moisture**. It feels softer too.

In the United States, seven billion rolls of toilet paper are sold every year. Each person uses about 140 rolls! What would we do without toilet paper?

# Early Bathroom Behavior

Before toilets, people used **chamber pots**. They emptied them into streams or sometimes the streets! People wiped with shells or leaves. They washed themselves with water or snow. Some people saved bits of cloth. They used these to clean their bottoms.

a chamber pot

Ancient Romans had public toilets. These were stone blocks with holes. People cleaned themselves with a sponge on a stick. Everyone used the same one!

**Public toilets in ancient Rome had multiple seats.**

The Chinese were using toilet paper in the 500s CE. By the 1300s, they produced 10 million packages a year.

Other countries were slower to catch on. In the 1700s, Americans still used outdoor bathrooms. These **outhouses** had no toilet paper. Some people cleaned themselves with corn cobs! Printed newspapers and magazines were also used.

an outhouse

a bidet

Some countries had other ideas. The French invented the **bidet** in 1710. This little washtub cleaned a person's bottom.

In 1857, Joseph Gayetty sold the first American toilet paper. It came in packages of 500 folded sheets. Each package cost 50 cents!

Joseph Gayetty

A man named Seth Wheeler thought toilet paper should be rolled. That's how his company made wrapping paper. Brothers Clarence and E. Irvin Scott liked this idea. They began making rolls of Scott toilet tissue in 1890.

Early toilet paper wasn't soft or smooth. It took many years for it to get better. In the 1930s, one ad said toilet paper was "splinter-free."

# From Forest to Factory

How is toilet paper made today? It starts in a forest or tree farm. People operate powerful machines. The machines cut down trees. They strip off the branches and divide the trees into logs.

Large machines can move many logs at a time.

The logs are sent to a factory. There, they are prepared. Bark is removed. Then the logs go to a machine called a chipper. It has a spinning blade. It cuts the logs into small pieces.

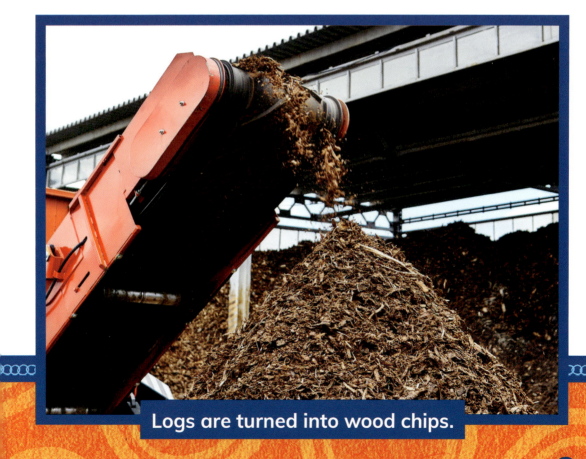

Logs are turned into wood chips.

Pulp moves through machinery at a factory.

Next, the wood chips are mixed with **chemicals**. This mixture is heated. It cooks for three hours. The mixture turns to mush. Now it is called **pulp**.

The pulp is cleaned and bleached. **Lignin** must be removed. This is a sticky material. It is like a glue that holds the wood fibers together. If it was not removed, the toilet paper would not be as strong. It could turn yellow.

A pulp and paper factory

Water is added to the pulp. This makes paper stock. It is sprayed onto a screen. Most of the water drains off. A thin layer of paper is left. But it is still wet.

Thin layers of paper are rolled.

Toilet paper starts off as very large rolls.

The thin layer of paper goes into a drying machine. Hot steam removes the moisture. A machine with a metal blade scrapes the paper off the dryer. It is rolled onto a huge **spool**. One spool can hold about 50 miles (80.5 kilometers) of toilet paper!

Tiny holes are added to the toilet paper.

A machine removes the giant roll. The paper passes over a roller with raised bumps. These bumps make a pattern. Another roller has pins. The pins make tiny holes. Holes make the paper easier to tear into sheets.

Next, the paper is wrapped around a cardboard tube. A saw slices the tube into smaller rolls. Most are packed in bundles and wrapped in plastic.

Finally, toilet paper is ready to leave the factory. Trucks deliver it to stores and warehouses.

**Trucks are loaded at factories.**

# Earth-Friendly Toilet Paper

Each day, 27,000 trees are cut down to make toilet paper. This destroys animal homes. New trees may be planted. But they take a long time to grow. People need trees too. Trees produce **oxygen**. We need this to breathe.

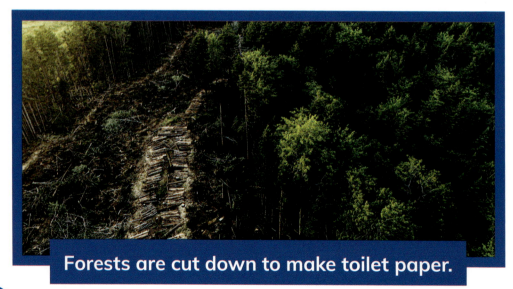
Forests are cut down to make toilet paper.

Paper is sorted at a recycling center.

But not all toilet paper comes from trees. Some comes from recycled paper. Mail, magazines, and newspapers can all be used to make toilet paper. This is better for the environment. So how is recycled toilet paper made?

Used paper is dumped into a pulping machine. This machine removes staples and paper clips. It is filled with warm water. The paper turns to pulp.

Machines sort and clean used paper.

A paper production machine

Next the color must be removed. Air is added to the pulp. Ink from the paper sticks to air bubbles. The bubbles float to the top.

After the ink is removed, the pulp is dried. The dry paper is bleached. This turns it white.

A bamboo forest

Recycled paper saves trees. There are also other ways to protect the earth. Toilet paper can be made from **bamboo**. It grows faster than trees. In fact, bamboo is the fastest growing plant on the planet! It needs less land and water.

Toilet paper can also come from sugarcane. This plant is already grown for sugar. Using sugarcane means fewer trees will be cut down.

**A truck harvests sugarcane.**

# Make Your Own Toilet Paper Planters

You can make Earth-friendly planters using toilet paper rolls. They can be placed directly in the ground. The cardboard roll will break down into tiny pieces and become part of the earth. Try this fun activity with your friends and a grown-up.

## What You Need:

- a carboard toilet paper roll
- scissors
- soil or potting mix for planting
- a flower or vegetable seed or cutting from a plant

## What You Do:

1. Cut your toilet paper roll in half so you have two planters.

2. On one end of the tube, make four 1/2-inch (1.3-centimeter) cuts. (Make sure cuts are evenly spaced.) You should end up with four flaps. Repeat on the other toilet paper roll.

3. Fold each flap toward the center of the tube one at a time. (It helps to work in a clockwise direction.)

4. Tuck the last flap under the first. Your planter should now have a flat bottom.

5. Add soil until your planter is about 3/4 full.

6. Plant your cutting or seed.

7. Place your planter in a sunny spot and wait for your seed to sprout. (You can also plant it directly in your garden.) Don't forget to water!

# Glossary

**bamboo** (bam-BOO)—a tropical grass with a hard, hollow stem

**bidet** (bih-DAY)—a bathroom fixture with a faucet that is used to wash a person's bottom

**chamber pot** (CHAYM-buhr POT)—a type of bowl that people used as a toilet

**chemical** (KE-muh-kuhl)—a substance used in or produced by chemistry; medicines, gunpowder, and food preservatives all are made from chemicals.

**hygiene** (HAHY-jeen)—the practice of keeping yourself and your surroundings clean

**lignin** (LIG-nin)—a substance that occurs in the woody cell walls of plants and in the cementing material between them

**moisture** (MOIS-chuhr)—wetness

**outhouse** (OUT-hows)—a small, outdoor bathroom

**oxygen** (OK-suh-juhn)—a colorless gas in the air that people and animals need to breathe

**ply** (PLAHY)—one of the folds, layers, or strands of which something, such as toilet paper, is made up

**pulp** (PUHLP)—a mixture of ground-up paper and water

**spool** (SPOOL)—a wheel on which toilet paper is wound

# Read More

Briggs, Korwin. *The Invention Hunters Discover How Machines Work*. New York: Little, Brown and Company, 2019.

Gholz, Sophia. *A History of Toilet Paper (and Other Potty Tools)*. Philadelphia: Running Press Kids, 2022.

Murray, Julie. *Best Inventions: Toilet*. Minneapolis: Abdo Zoom, 2023.

# Internet Sites

*Kidadl: 57 Fun Toilet Paper Facts That Will Make You Laugh Out Loud*
kidadl.com/facts/fun-toilet-paper-facts-that-will-make-you-laugh-out-loud

*Kiddle: Toilet Paper Facts for Kids*
kids.kiddle.co/Toilet_paper

*Toilet Paper History: The Toilet Paper Manufacturing Process*
toiletpaperhistory.net/toilet-paper-made/how-is-toilet-paper-made/

# Index

amount used, 7
bamboo, 26
bidets, 11
chamber pots, 8
China, 10
early bathrooms, 8, 9, 10
early toilet paper, 8, 9, 10, 12, 13
factories, 14, 15, 16, 17, 21
forests, 14, 22
France, 11
Gayetty, Joseph, 12
lignin, 17

machinery, 14, 16, 19, 20, 24
outhouses, 10
oxygen, 22
plies, 6
public toilets, 9
pulp, 16, 17, 18, 24, 25
recycled paper, 23, 24, 26
Scott toilet tissue, 13
sugarcane, 27
trees, 14, 22, 23, 26, 27
Wheeler, Seth, 13

# About the Author

A public and a school librarian, Gloria Koster belongs to the Children's Book Committee of Bank Street College of Education. She enjoys both city and country life, dividing her time between Manhattan and the small town of Pound Ridge, New York. Gloria has three adult children and a bunch of energetic grandkids.